LIFE
BEHIND
HIS SHIELD

LIFE
BEHIND
HIS SHIELD

A Daughter's Life with Her Father,
a Police Officer

MEGHAN ALANIS

WestBow
PRESS
A DIVISION OF THOMAS NELSON

WestBow Press books may be ordered through
booksellers or by contacting:

WestBow Press
A Division of Thomas Nelson
1663 Liberty Drive
Bloomington, IN 47403
www.westbowpress.com
1-(866) 928-1240

ISBN: 978-1-4497-8811-7 (e)
ISBN: 978-1-4497-8812-4 (sc)

Library of Congress Control Number: 2013904710

Printed in the United States of America

WestBow Press rev. date: 3/20/2013

To my father, Gaylon. With selflessness and bravery,
he serves God, his family, and his community.
I pray to be a little more like him in all I do.

TABLE OF CONTENTS

FOREWORD

When a loved one is daily exposed to possible peril, it is difficult to ignore the fact that each goodbye may be the final one. In *Life Behind his Shield,* Meghan Alanis examines the angst she felt growing up as a police officer's daughter. She relates how she kept quiet about the anxiety she faced each day, and how she tried to "be strong" and obtain control over her life with perfectionistic behaviors.

Worry appears to be one of our strongest human tendencies. The Bible talks profusely about anxiety and overcoming fear. Even Christ Himself addressed fear and anxiety in 365 verses. Many people spend their lives worrying about the "what ifs" of situations, and if these anxious feelings are suppressed without the individual addressing them, it can set the stage for anxiety disorders to develop.

Over time Meghan learned that she needed to express her feelings and process them with her counselors and family members. Gaining a realization that God is in control can relieve anxiety, in that we can trust Him with our daily needs, no matter how small or great.

I would recommend this book to family members of those who serve to protect the people of their community or country. I am convinced that they will identify with Meghan's story, and will be able to glean comfort and help from her experiences. I also would recommend that those heroes who serve in the protection of others read this book, to gain insight into how their job affects their loved ones and to open conversations about this subject with their families.

Nancy C. Albers, Ph.D.
Clinical Psychologist
Fresno, California
2013

INTRODUCTION

So many families live with a parent who serves in some type of service role, especially armed forces. Children and spouses of police officers, firefighters, and members of the armed forces all live in a different world than everyone else.

From the outside looking in, our families appear happy normal. They typically make good money, live in beautiful houses in good school districts, wear nice clothes, and drive fancy cars. Thanks to the overtime that many police officers and firefighters work, many of our families enjoy exotic vacations, boating, skiing, and other pricey activities. Our moms or dads usually have great stories to tell, and everyone wants him or her to talk at barbecues.

It is kind of fun actually to have the cool parent, the father or mother who:

- Has little kids looking up to him or her and dreaming about being in his or her line of work.

- Knows everything that goes on in your hometown.
- Knows a lot about guns or how to fight fires.
- Essentially has a key to the city and wears a uniform to work.

Who wouldn't want a superhero for a parent? What kid wouldn't love that?

There are so many positives to having a superhero for a parent, but unfortunately, there are great costs as well. Spouses and children often deal with stress, anxiety, and depression a little bit more than the average family. They feel they are consistently out of control when it comes to their spouse's or parent's safety, so they grasp for anything to give them hope. God willing, they cling to a faith that is bigger than all of them, a Lord who doesn't ensure sunshine and rainbows every day but does promise to not give us more than we can handle. Or perhaps, like I did as a child, my faith was not fully matured, so to deal with the anxiety and lack of control when it came to my dad coming home safe after his shift, I overcompensated in all other areas of my life. I overachieved in everything from school assignments, my behavior and how I acted at home. I remember being in elementary school and I received a B on an assignment. This was the first B I had ever received in my life and you would have thought I was going to die. If I wasn't perfect, getting A's on report cards and being the teacher's favorite student, then I wasn't in control. If

I didn't do my chores and received a punishment then I again, wasn't perfect. I prayed and hoped that, if I could control every detail of my life, there would be enough stability to bring him home each morning.

My father has been a police officer for almost thirty years. This is a story about my life growing up in his household, the good and bad times; the events that made my mom, sister, and me beam with pride; and the happenings that made us pray like crazy that he was going to come home to us. I hope you can relate, especially if you have a parent who is a police officer. Even if you don't, I believe that families of firefighters and those in the armed forces may experience many of the same things. Or perhaps if you didn't grow up with a parent who put their life on the line every time he or she went to work, maybe you would be inspired to extend grace to the families who risk it all to keep others safe.

CHAPTER 1

The Early Years

I know it's a little controversial when it comes to how far back people can recall memories. My husband swears he doesn't remember anything before kindergarten. I, on the other hand, remember way further back than that.

On my third birthday, I woke up in red sweats that were decorated with puff paints. I went into my parents' room, where they were still asleep under their faded, pale-blue sheets and comforter. I crawled into bed, and they made a "Meghan Sandwich," snuggling me in between them for as long as I wanted.

My childhood memories are, for the most part, wonderful. We were the standard upper-middle-class, suburban, nuclear family with mom, dad, two daughters, and slew of pets that came and went. We had great vacations over summer. We did family nights every week, and for the most part, we were really involved in each other's lives.

I grew accustomed to uniqueness quickly because my parents always worked odd hours. For a long time, my dad, the police officer, worked nights while my corporate mom worked days. He would sleep during the day but wake up in time to pick us up from school. I really didn't know this was different from other families until I went to school and experienced friends and their families.

You mean it wasn't normal for dads to be gone all night?

I had absolutely no clue what my dad actually did when he went to work. I knew he was a police officer. I knew he wore a uniform. But that was about it. I didn't know if he drank coffee and ate donuts his entire shift or if he rescued kittens out of trees and helped old people cross the street. My mind could only imagine. We lived in a very conservative, quiet neighborhood, so the idea of crime was foreign to me.

In my sheltered world, I did have odd encounters with my dad where the image of what he did for a living didn't add up. I pictured him always being safe on the job and never being in any actual real danger. But one morning, I woke up, stumbled out of bed, and made my way to the breakfast table. My mom, dad, older sister, and (possibly) my aunt were already seated. Everything seemed normal, just another day of eating together as a family. It must have been a Saturday.

As I ate, I realized something was different. I was still groggy from just waking up, but as I glanced around the table, I realized everyone was quiet, except my mom. She was crying. I immediately looked around to figure out what was going on, and then I focused on my dad for a moment. He had stitches above his eye.

How did he get those? What in the world could have caused this?

I have vague memories of my dad telling the story to other family members. It was no big deal. He just got in a little fight with a drunk guy, and before my dad could get out his baton, the guy got off a cheap shot and hit my dad's eye. I don't recall how many stitches were across his eyebrow, but it seemed like a lot at the time.

So my image of what my dad really did as a police officer and what I thought he did began to shatter. It wasn't immediate, but there were definitely some cracks in it by now. My little mind couldn't even fathom my dad being in danger, and now he was injured between the time he left for work the night prior and this morning at the breakfast table. I was safely and soundly asleep all night, and my dad was getting stitches. That was so hard for me to understand.

Furthermore, I really couldn't even picture my dad being in a fight with someone. My dad is the epitome of a loving, mushy-gushy dad. He raised two daughters, and he was involved in everything we did. When I say mushy-gushy, I mean extremely tender about all things regarding us girls. When my mom was at work during the day, my dad would come to our elementary school and be a room mom. He would assist with arts and crafts and help plan holiday parties, all with the other stay-at-home moms. He didn't care one bit. He was all in. He would play dolls, color, or watch movies with us. He'd do pretty much anything we wanted to keep us happy. So how could this tenderhearted, gentle man get in a wrestling match with someone? It just didn't add up.

I think this was the beginning of the end of me feeling like I was safe. All of the sudden, I realized that things weren't as they seemed, and I wasn't in control. There was now risk associated with my dad leaving to go to work, and that made me nervous. Looking back, I can see all of this, but at the time, I couldn't put it into words. I just knew I began to dread my dad backing out of the driveway each evening to head to the substation. I would no longer sleep safely and soundly because I began to fear what might be happening to my dad while he was across town.

I still had many more years of living in my bubble in regards to safety, the world, crime, and my dad's role in it. However, rather than dealing with it at that time, I began to stuff it deeper and deeper into the core of who I was so I could still try to imagine that my dad was always safe. But we all know that feelings, emotions, fears, and anxieties can't stay buried forever.

To try to conceal how I was really feeling, I became an elementary school-aged control freak. From grades to behavior to anything I could produce, I would excel. I could control these things in this big, crazy world, so that helped me cope. Little did I know I was creating scars that would stay with me to this very day.

CHAPTER 2

Growing Up

Other than the increased anxiety and worries I carried around, growing up in my house felt like every other kid's experience. There was always lots of laughter, love, and joy. With three females in the house (my mom, my sister, and myself), conflicts were loud and energetic. Once puberty hit our home, there was a lot of drama and more tears than usual, but overall, our family was fun, and all my school years were enjoyable.

Until I could figure out that I felt scared because of my dad's job, I put up that mask that I thought his job was really awesome. Honestly, I think one advantage that all children of service people have over other kids, especially in the early years, is the best show-and-tell items. Having a parent who wears a uniform and badge for a living does have its costs, but when you're little, there is a time period when his or her line of work is pretty incredible.

For show-and-tell, I brought awards my dad received, badges, and pictures. There was no greater feeling like having your classmates *ooh* and *ahh* over your dad's profession. They thought it was so cool that he was in the newspaper or on last night's news.

Even though there was always the anxieties that you buried every time your parent went to work, there was a sense of pride that began to well up, knowing you had the parent who everyone wished he or she had. Learning to perfect the mask of pride when you are really angry and terrified at his or her profession is a skill that families of service people must do. Nobody wants to hear about the reality of living with a parent who comes home with injuries or gets home late after a shift because he or she had to write a report for a fatal car accident. People want to hear the stories—not the effects they have on the loved ones surrounding them.

My dad had the opportunity to wear many different hats during his time with the department. From riding motorcycles, being a part of violent crime units, training, and having a police dog, he told us many stories over dinner. Along with those tales came many opportunities for him to come to my school and share. My teachers would jump at the chance to have him come by in uniform to talk about what he does for a living, how to be safe at school and home, and many other topics. When he had a police dog, he would come to the schools, show the kids how well the dog was trained, and talk about how they were partners.

What's funny is that, during these times, having a dad as a police officer was really great. Although many times I felt like I was wearing a mask, I also thought it was so neat to bring him to school and show him off. It really seemed like everyone wished his or her dad had a job like mine did. They wished that their dad had the stories, gadgets, and guns to share with their classmates. For the first time in long time, I realized I had something that other people envied, and to a young child, that felt somewhat good.

Especially in the depths of the insecurities, it was nice to attempt to fill it with popularity. I had the cool parent, and people only wished that their life was like mine. Little did they know, all the great stories came with a lot of baggage.

For example, I bet my classmates didn't know that:

- My dad was a police officer 24/7, not just when he went to work.
- Even the most innocent of occasions could turn into an episode of *Cops* at any given moment.

A family vacation we took one summer was memorable. My parents were so good at creating fun memories over the summer, and many of those were created at the beach. It was nothing flashy, just spending time at the ocean, eating out, and sleeping in late in a big hotel bed. Most of these times were priceless.

We were headed home one evening in our family station wagon from the Central Coast. My sister and I were dozing in and out of sleep in the backseat, and we had packed our car with luggage, pillows, sand toys, and all the loot we were coming home with. It was a great trip. While cruising down the highway, I heard my dad get on our car phone. I didn't know who he was calling and in regards to what, but I heard him start describing the car in front of us. He gave the color, make, model, and license plate number. Being too little to understand what was going on, I didn't really pay any attention to it.

My dad remained on the phone with someone, which I now know was dispatch for the local police department he worked for. I heard him say things like his badge number and other letters and numbers I didn't quite understand. We continued driving for some time. It occurred to me that we were now following this car. When he changed lanes, we did. When he sped up or slowed down, we did. Finally, he exited the freeway, and my dad followed right behind him.

Before I knew it, we were pulling into an undesirable part of town. It was dark outside, but the lights of the city were bright as I looked out the window into a part of our city that I had never seen before. I noticed we were still following the vehicle in front of us. I was startled to see two or three cop cars come up behind us, speed around, and pull over the vehicle that we had been following. Their sirens were loud, and their blue and red lights were bright.

What is going on?

I looked around the car at my older sister next to me and my mom in the front seat, searching and seeking for some acknowledgment as to what was taking place. I peered around the front seat of the car to see uniformed officers emerge from their cars and surround the suspect's vehicle. It was now at a complete stop in front of us. They pulled a man out of the car and placed him into handcuffs.

Just then, my dad said, "I'll be right back."

He got out of our car. As the other uniformed officers were walking the man in handcuffs back to their squad cars, my dad approached them and started smiling, shaking hands, and making jokes. My dad was not in uniform. Our family car was in the middle of all of this mess, and my mom, sister, and I were sitting like ducks in the middle of a pond, watching from inside our station wagon. The police walked the arrested man right past our car. To this day, I could tell you what he was wearing and what he looked like.

Could he remember the same details about me?

When I grew up and became an adult, I asked my dad about this situation.

I asked, "Dad? Could you explain to me what happened when we followed that guy into Chinatown when we were coming home from the coast?"

"You remember that?" He replied. My silence was his answer.

My dad continued, "well, you may not know this because you were so little, but I noticed the vehicle in front of us swerving and driving uncontrollably on the road. I followed him for sometime and recognized his behavior to be that of a drunk driver. I knew if he continued driving he was putting himself at risk and others on the road at risk, so I called my department and gave them our location so officers could come out, pull him over, and arrest him."

"When you say he was drunk, how drunk was he?" I asked.

"He could barely walk to the patrol car when he was handcuffed. He was extremely intoxicated," said my dad.

I had to ask because I had wondered my whole life, so I asked, "Dad, why did you get out of the car that night?"

My dad pondered the question and then answered, "well the officers that arrived at the scene were friends of mine. I of course wanted to say hello to them, as well as give them the details of how long I was following the car, etc. That's all."

Now, as an adult and parent myself, I can understand this situation as noble and brave. Perhaps my dad saved a life that night. Maybe this man was going to harm someone or himself. Because my dad had the patience, knowledge, and skill to call and get some help, this man was brought to justice, and the streets were a little bit safer that evening.

Hindsight is always twenty-twenty, and especially now, after so many years have passed, I can look back on this event with pride and adoration for my dad. But these are not the feelings I experienced as the little girl sitting in that backseat so many years ago.

As an innocent little girl, I felt completely vulnerable sitting there. We were in a part of town I had never seen before, just sitting in our family car, and my dad was in street clothes, not a uniform. I felt like we had been exposed. The arrested man saw my entire family and our license plate number.

Would he remember us? Would he remember the white guy in the station wagon who followed him and ultimately got him arrested? Would he want revenge?

He didn't know my dad was a cop. My dad wasn't in uniform that night. He was just an average Joe, driving his family back from the beach.

That experience as a family only further burst the little safety bubble that I tried to live in and find comfort in. It wouldn't be until much later that I could process this event in counseling and find peace and hope in my Lord and Savior. But at that moment, I felt like we would live the rest of our lives in a fishbowl. Any bad guy my dad arrested would follow him home, and anyone who was brought to justice at the hand of my father would seek retaliation on him and our family. At least, that is what my sweet, little, innocent brain thought.

I obviously didn't understand what my dad was actually doing when he went to work and how safe and protected he was/is. All I knew was this was just another facet of this life that I could not control. I did not know the Lord yet, so rather than speak up and ask for help from my family or my faith, I continued to burn into my core belief that this world was not safe and I would become a victim myself if I were not always in control. My poor, precious soul was so troubled at a young age. This was so much to carry and take on.

At times, my anxiety would bubble up, and I would have a meltdown, as I affectionately called it. My parents started to get concerned when I would sob uncontrollably because I got a B, not an A, on an assignment. Or being told I couldn't do something I really wanted to do would cause me to erupt in anger and become violent.

Before I even entered junior high school, I saw a child counselor twice. Very sweet people tried to get to the bottom of my need to achieve and excel, but unfortunately, they could just offer temporary solutions to a much bigger and deeper issue. I still had a lot of life and experiences to go through before I could offer this whole mess up to the Lord and truly be free.

In his grace and timing, the Lord would use a nationwide tragedy to remove the veil from my eyes and begin to walk me down the road to recovery. Through a little more pain, I would soon find healing and redemption from the prison of anxiety that I had been living in for too long.

CHAPTER 3

My New Reality

It was the fall semester of my senior year of high school when September 11 changed our nation forever. I remember that morning and every detail, much like every other American. I live on the West Coast so it was much earlier here when the first plane hit. My mom was baking cookies for some event that day, and I was stumbling out of bed when our phone rang. It was my sister.

"Hello?" my mom answered.

"Are you watching the news?" Sara asked. "New York has been attacked."

Just then, my mom and I stopped what we were doing and sat staring at our television. We watched in horror and disbelief at what was happening. The images were so frightening—flames shooting from the sides of the Twin Towers and people jumping from high floors in an effort to avoid burning to death. New Yorkers near ground zero literally ran for their lives, pausing occasionally to stop and look back, as if to confirm what was really happening.

Another detail in the images splattered across our TV screen was the droves of emergency vehicles driving toward the burning buildings. Everyone else was running away from the disaster, but some people were running to it. Fire trucks, ambulances, and police cars were screaming Code 3 toward the Twin Towers.

Here are these men and women racing toward the Twin Towers in hopes to save just one person from a horrible death when they were really running to their own. Who would have known that the Twin Towers were about to fall?

What I saw disturbed me, and I rested in the comfort that the attack was far away from me. I went to school expecting just a normal day that started in a horrible way. I was surprised to encounter the quietness and numbness that I did on my high school campus. All my teachers canceled their lesson plans, and we just sat and continued to stare at the TV screen. We saw image after image of men and women covered in ash and dust after the Twin Towers fell. Fire trucks and police cars were mangled in the mess as debris crushed the metal as if the cars were soda cans. These pictures flooded my mind, and it wasn't until a few days later that I knew my life would never be the same.

In the wake of September 11, I continued to process everything that had just happened to our nation. I watched the news every day to hear if they found any more survivors and if the death toll had been raised. It began to occur to me that America would never be the same. I would never walk a family member to the gate of his or her flight and watch the plane take off from the window. I would never again travel to New York and see those identical Twin Towers completing that famous skyline.

My anxiety rose as I realized that the disaster of America being attacked in New York wasn't as far away as I thought. I don't know why or how, but an idea hit me like a freight train.

If a terrorist attacked my town, everyone I know and love would be running for his or her life—sprinting for safety away from the disaster. But not everyone. My dad would be racing toward the disaster. He would be running for his life to the flames and smoke, hurrying with all he had in hopes to save one life. He would be rolling Code 3 toward the chaos while my mom, sister, and I waited and prayed.

This was my new reality. I don't know why it took me until my seventeenth year of life to realize this is what my dad did for a living. I think the false images of him just writing speeding tickets, going to elementary schools to talk about safety, and looking handsome in his uniform was what I chose to believe about my dad. Yes, he was a police officer and carried a gun, baton, and handcuffs.

But that doesn't mean he ever used them? Right?

My idea of what an actual police officer did on the job and how my dad operated were two very different things until now. It never occurred to me that my dad was risking his life every time he backed out of the driveway. If my town were attacked, there was a good chance we would lose him in the process. Not only did September 11 take off my blinders regarding the safety and security of our nation, it changed how I looked at my dad.

I know this sounds naïve, but I believe this is how I coped with his profession for so long. It was always easier to think of what he did as cool rather than dangerous, what it really was. It was always easier to bury the worry and anxiety and be an overachiever in all other areas of my life than to face the reality I was living in.

If disaster struck, a criminal decided to open fire on officers, or a routine call turned ugly, my dad would be in danger. He would sacrifice his life for the greater good, that is, for the safety of others and our city. My family and I would walk away from a casket with a folded-up flag rather than someone else. It would be a twenty-one gun salute for him, not a stranger. These realizations were overwhelming for me.

Why have I pretended so long? Why didn't I allow myself to see my dad's profession for what it really was? Why have I never been able to see servicepeople as extraordinary people who risked their lives daily for others? Why was I so naïve to think that all they did was drive around and write tickets, hang around a firehouse and eat chili, or work on base doing hours of training but never actually have to go to combat?

It was as if all of the fears and worries I had stuffed down for the so long were all rushing to the surface. You would think that new self-discovery would create an immense pride within me for these men, women, and my dad. You would think that I could see truly see the heroism in their professions and trust the rest to God.

However, it was the complete opposite. A deep-seated anger began to swell up in me. I'm not proud of this feeling, and really at the bottom of it all is extreme selfishness because I was only thinking about how the risk my dad placed himself in affected me. If I were completely honest, I was just angry. I was livid at my dad for risking his life for other people when that would mean robbing us of a lifetime with him. The idea of him running toward a burning building or gunfire infuriated me because he should be running home to his wife and daughters.

Why would he put his life on the line for total strangers and, at the same time, risk missing out on all of life's experiences with us?

I quickly learned that a cost of burying anxiety and worry for so long is that anger is the secondary emotion that helps it stay buried. I had this overwhelming feeling of anger at my dad for choosing this profession, God for allowing the world to get this bad, and myself for feeling that I was no longer safe. This only further caused me to believe that, if I did not remain in control 100 percent of the time, something horrible would happen.

Furthermore, my choice not to deal with the anxiety I

was feeling, as a result of my anger, led me to have panic attacks. Situations where I felt stuck or like I was unable to leave without causing a scene sent my pulse racing and breaths to shorten. I was a mess.

I believed in God at this point in my life (and still do), and I had even pursued a relationship with Jesus Christ. For some reason, this even felt bigger than He was. I felt like, if I prayed or reached out for help, even the Lord Almighty couldn't save me from this pit I was in. It was just easier to try to be in control all on my own and be very purposeful in every decision I made. My false theology that God could not protect me from the evil in this world robbed me of so much in my life, especially joy. Instead of dealing with my worries and fears, I was essentially giving into the power of them. Evil was winning in my life. I just didn't realize it. I was about to go to college and enter into some of the most exciting years in a young person's life, but fear and panic attacks paralyzed me.

I wanted help, but I no longer trusted the counseling process because it didn't help me when I was a child. I tried relying on God, but I felt like I needed something or someone tangible to give me safety, and my heart just didn't feel like God could do that. So unfortunately, I stayed stuck, unable and unwilling to seek health until my heavenly father loving and graciously caused me and my entire family to look at the pain and fear that had been holding us captive for so many years regarding my dad's career.

CHAPTER 4

The Fire

I wish I could say that everything surrounding my dad and his career began to get easier to live with after September 11. I wish I could say that, if by some miracle, my family and I would come to grips with his profession and the danger that he put himself in on a daily basis. Unfortunately, it was the complete opposite.

As I continued into adulthood, I only became more aware of how different our family was. When I was little, I loved how other kids wished their dad was as cool as mine was, but as an adult, I would give anything to have a dad who was an accountant, plumber, or anything else that seemed run-of-the-mill and the farthest thing from dangerous. I didn't understand how a person's profession could carry so much power over someone.

Along with these new and continued realizations about my dad, my anxiety only continued to grow. Memories of how I felt as that little girl sitting in our family station wagon in the middle of town, watching a handcuffed man walk right by me, flooded my heart and mind. These memories began to gain so much power over me that I continued to have more and more panic attacks, which were beginning to run my life. Unfortunately, I didn't realize how immobile and nonfunctioning I had become. I eventually just became afraid of life around me, leading me almost to agoraphobia. Agoraphobia as a type of anxiety disorder in which you avoid situation that you're afraid might cause you panic. You might avoid being alone, leaving your home, or any situation where you could feel trapped, embarrassed or helpless if you do panic. This describes how I was feeling perfectly. It was just easier to stay home, where it was safe and I was in control. If I left, then I might have a panic attack or become a victim because crime and violence is all around us. Right?

I was missing out on so much life around me, but my fear was crippling. I began to feel crazy because I assumed no one around me felt the same way. Everyone was living life, full of joy and excitement, and yet to me, the idea of going out, traveling, or allowing others to be in control literally made me sick. I was trapped and didn't realize how bad it had become.

I still lived at home while I was attending college, and although our busy lives kept us from seeing a lot of each other, my parents began to notice the changes in me. They realized how bad it become during a quick trip to the Bay Area to see a professional football game. In order to get to our seats at the stadium, we had to get on this massive escalator that I swear went up to the sky. Thousands of people were waiting to get on this thing. As we walked closer to it, I literally could no longer breathe.

I'm supposed to stand on that thing? What if it stops and I only make it halfway? Look how high up in the air that thing goes! What if I want to get off and I can't because there are so many people? I would be trapped!

All these thoughts flooded my mind. So as my family boarded the escalator, my sweet boyfriend walked up an obscene amount of stairs with me. Although I was tired and winded from the hike upstairs, I was in control. I could turn around and walk down if I needed to. I was free. My mom, looking at me as if to say, "We need to talk about what just happened," met me at the top of the stairs.

I slowly began to open up to my parents and my boyfriend (who is now my husband). I think everyone was a little taken back by how long I had been feeling this way and how bad everything had become. Everyone was a little shocked at how good an actress I was, but they were also sad that I felt like I had to wear my mask of "everything is fine" around them.

Why hadn't I said something sooner?

My family encouraged me to seek help. I think no one really knew what to do with me and didn't understand my paralyzed state, so they figured the problem was bigger than they were. I tried counseling a few times as an adult, but at the time, I didn't have the energy or strength to really deal with what was going on.

I was in the middle of college. I was working part time and realizing this cute boy I had been dating for a while was the man I would marry. My life was falling into place. Everything seemed to be going, just as the little girl version of myself had hoped.

Why would I want to drudge up the past and deal with my past in counseling?

Instead, I did a few sessions and decided I could deal with this myself and it should just get better. That was essentially like putting a Band-Aid on a gunshot wound. Unfortunately, the wounds of fear and anxiety were running so deep that talk therapy couldn't really touch it. I don't think I was ready to really acknowledge that I had been growing up scared of the world around me and fearing that God wouldn't be able to stop something horrible from happening to my family. I couldn't engage with how false my theology was about my heavenly father.

It was just easier to keep everything in the dark. I really began to believe that I would just always struggle with anxiety and fear. I figured that most people have things about themselves that they wished they could change, and this was mine. For the rest of my life I would fight this battle. I didn't believe that God was big enough, powerful enough, or cared enough to free me from my struggles. It was as though I had become the God of my life, and as long as I was in control, then everyone around me would be safe.

I don't think the God of the universe liked me thinking I was more powerful than He was. The more I stuffed the feelings and anxieties down, God kept bubbling them back up. He forced me to look at the fear, stress, and anger I had been swallowing for so long regarding my dad's profession.

I was stubborn, so it wasn't until late 2003 and early 2004 that the Lord forced my family and me to deal openly and honestly with what we all had been keeping a secret from each other for so long. In the meantime, life would continue to happen all around me, and before I knew it, it was Christmastime again. I was hoping to get lost in the lights, merriment, and hustle and bustle around me.

The Christmas season is always a time of fun, thankfulness, and laughter in our home. Of course, that time of year is a little crazy, so to have some downtime as a busy college student was almost priceless. Just two days after Christmas in 2003, my mom and I were lounging and watching a movie at home. The excitement of the holiday season was behind us, so a relaxing day at home was absolutely perfect. My dad was now working a day shift and usually got home in the late afternoon, so we were soaking up time, just the two of us.

Around lunchtime, we heard our back door open and close. We weren't really expecting anyone. We looked at each other and figured it had to have been my dad, but he wasn't due home for a few more hours.

My mom hollered out his name. He answered as he emerged into the room. His appearance shocked us. A black substance that looked like soot covered his face and hands. His patches on his uniform, usually bright white stars, were dingy and also covered in what looked like soot. His face was still, and he was not his usual warm and welcoming self.

"Are you okay? What happened?" my mom asked.

"Yeah, yeah, I'm fine," my dad replied with little emotion. "There was a fire this morning in an apartment. I was near that location, so I went and helped."

His attitude was as if he were trying to convince us that it was no big deal. But we are not stupid. You went and helped with a fire, and soot covers you.

How close did you have to be to look like you do?

"What?" my mom and I exclaimed. "Did you go into the fire? What do you mean helped?"

I think he realized we were both on to him, and he simply said he was going to change out of his uniform. He disappeared down the hall. My mom followed him, but I stayed put. I knew in my gut that something was wrong. My own fear and anxiety of seeing my dad hurt or upset left me immobile. I muted our movie, hoping I might hear my dad explain to my mom what happened, but unfortunately, I heard the worst sound of all.

From the other side of the house, I heard my dad crying. He wept as he told my mom what happened that morning in the fire. I couldn't make out the details, but I knew that whatever my dad experienced was beyond traumatic. While I waited for one of them to come back down the hall, I sat and just prayed.

The sound of the shower turning on in the back of the house broke the silence. My mom came down the hall and looked as if she had been crying as well.

"What happened?" I asked.

My mom slowly began to speak, "Just like your dad said, he heard a call come out over the radio of an apartment fire. He just so happened to be near that location so he rolled on the call. He was so close in fact, that he beat the fire department there."

She paused a took a deep breath, "Upon arriving he heard people shouting that there was a young woman trapped inside the apartment. Without hesitation he ran in to look for her."

My mom paused and her eyes filled with tears, "She was badly burned by the time your daddy found her. He reached out to grab her hand, and as he pulled her to bring her out, her skin came off in his hand."

My mom cried quietly while I just sat in shock. My mind could not begin to imagine what that must have been like.

"Did she make it out of the fire?" I asked.

"Yes, she survived, because your daddy carried her out," said my mom.

All of this information was so much to take in. I was just beginning to deal with the dangers that my dad encountered on his job, as a policeman. Now, he's running into burning apartments. No oxygen mask, no fire suit or helmet, just him and black smoke. He risked his own life to save that young woman's.

My dad later shared with my mom that, as he sat in the back of an ambulance while the firefighters put out the flames, he was told it was a miracle he survived. Being exposed to that much black smoke should have caused him to pass out so he must have had a guardian angel. He was taken to the hospital for a lung x-ray, but he was released and sent home for the rest of the day, which is why he got home around lunchtime that afternoon.

My dad would later receive a lifesaving medal for the role he played in this fire. He was actually nominated for a national lifesaving medal that the president would present. He received "Officer of the Year" from his department, and all the notoriety was overwhelming. We went to banquet after banquet where he was honored and applauded for his efforts.

Don't get me wrong. It was all amazing, and I was and still am so proud of him. His selflessness and bravery are qualities I can only pray to have a portion of in my life. However, in the midst of all of the standing ovations, our family kept quiet. We didn't know that we were all feeling the same. Of course, we were proud, but that underlying anger and fear for what could have happened in that apartment fire was lying dormant in all of us, and it was about to erupt.

This was the first time I realized that kids of other servicepeople—whether firefighters, corrections officers, armed forces members, and others—had to be feeling the same way I did. It didn't matter where your parent was going when he or she backed out of the driveway, whether it was a substation, firehouse, or base. Anytime your parent left to go put his or her life in danger for the sake of others, how could you not be afraid? Unless you had something bigger than you to cling to for hope and safety, how could you not want to control the world just to bring him or her home?

Unfortunately, our inability and unwillingness to deal with our feelings following the fire were again brought into the light just a few short months later. Not even three months after the roller coaster we were all on regarding my dad running into a burning apartment, an event so evil and so public took place. It again forced us to look at what my dad did on the job and how it affected all of us.

CHAPTER 5

The Call

On a Friday in 2004, I was in the spring semester of my sophomore year of college. I was still living at home. Our family was gearing up to have a busy weekend. My mom was going to be in a counseling class all weekend and pretty much unreachable, so my dad and I were supposed to fend for ourselves. My dad was still working day shift with his police dog, and he usually got home in the late afternoon.

I was working on homework and waiting for my dad to get home when I completely lost track of time. I got distracted from my work only because my stomach began to growl, so I looked at the clock to realize it was already after six o'clock.

That's weird. When Dad is late, he usually calls.

I tried his cell phone and left a message. I figured he probably got a late call, and I would see him soon. But more and more time passed, and I began to worry. My mom was still unreachable, and it was now after seven. A little late was one thing, but a three-hour delay was making me nervous.

Where is he?

To distract myself and keep me from calling his cell phone again, I turned on the television. I landed on the local news.

Eight o'clock on a Friday? That's weird.

I turned to the other local channels, and they were all saying the same thing. The breaking news was that the worst mass murder in the history of our town had happened. A man killed nine of his children, ranging from infants to young adults. All of the children were believed to be born of incest.

My heart sank.

How could this happen in my town? How did someone capable of something so heinous live within miles of me?

This was obviously a large crime scene. It looked like it all happened that afternoon, so I began to think that maybe my dad just went to help on this call.

Perhaps that is why he is late.

I tried his cell phone again and still didn't get an answer. Then I saw an image come across my TV screen that literally took my breath away. The first images of this man, this wicked and ugly man, were shown on the screen. He was being walked off his front porch in handcuffs, and the officer clicking the handcuffs into place and guiding him away from his house was my father. There on the news, on every local channel, was my dad standing with and guarding this man in blood-soaked clothing. My dad was no doubt in the presence of evil.

The time that followed this horrible event was kind of a blur. I waited for my dad to get home that evening, and I honestly didn't know what to expect. It was late by the time he got home, and while I waited, I just sat and stared at the images on my TV screen. I saw images of crime scene officers carrying body bags, bag after bag, out of the house. Many bags were the size of small children. Images were shown from inside the house, only shedding light on how completely disturbed this man was. An obsession with vampires and coffins filled his dark home.

How? And why? Why did this happen?

Watching my dad process this event was very difficult. I would later find out that the call went out to officers as a domestic disturbance because this man's wife and family were wanting all of the children who were inside the house. No big deal, right? My dad rolled on the call, thinking he would mediate a fight between a husband and wife and call it a day. He had no idea that, by the time he got there, this man would go back into his house and kill all of the children while officers were outside. My dad and many other officers struggled with the knowledge that the children were possibly murdered inside the house, on their watch, while they were right outside the house, trying to get in and save them.

This brought a lot of darkness to our home. This case was very public. Immediately following this event, my dad's picture was all over the news and online. He was on the cover of local and national newspapers. (Even when

I researched the details of the case as I wrote this, my father's picture is still associated with this event so many years later.)

I again felt like we were living in a fishbowl. Our town was mourning this horrible tragedy, and my father was grieving the fact that he couldn't save the children. My mom, sister, and I just stood and watched. As others looked into our family, we just continued to go through the motions, again saying nothing.

My dad didn't share too much about how he was dealing with this. I think he was trying to protect us girls, but unfortunately, his silence led my mom, sister, and I to fill in our own blanks. I had no idea how my dad was functioning. We didn't know how he could:

- Experience something so awful and just go back to work.
- Continue to allow himself to come in contact with such pain and such brokenness in our city.

Did what he see and interact with that day affect him? Was he scared? Was he sad?

I had no clue. I think we all felt God's prompting to talk about our feelings, but we were so used to swallowing hard and burying our fears and worries that we didn't know how to begin the conversation.

Also, I didn't know if I even wanted to know what my dad encountered and saw on the job. The crime, hate, evil, and sin that he saw and experienced in our town to this day breaks my heart. I didn't understand how he could:

- See so much darkness and yet come home to our little suburban neighborhood and love on his wife and daughters with a soft and gentle spirit
- Be exposed to everything on his job and yet still have hope in humanity

I think a part of me understood why he kept away details about his job from us girls.

How could you believe in good when you encounter so much bad?

However, after so many years and with my sister and I now being adults, our family knew it was time to start talking. We could no longer live in our silence and pretend we were all doing fine. In an effort to pursue health and fight for our family, we all leaned in and began to open up. Despite the awkwardness, the tears, and the fears and anger, it was time to start talking about how we were all feeling in regards to Dad being a police officer. We all knew the amazing life that it had afforded us, but we needed to deal with the costs.

Little did we know, us girls had all been feeling the same way for so long, just handling it in very different ways. By God's grace, we began talking, and we would eventually find the freedom we all craved for.

CHAPTER 6

Building Lines of Communication

In general, I think it's hard for families to talk about their feelings. When things are good, maybe it is a little easier, but during hard times, it often feels like it's difficult to be vulnerable. I would say that my family was exceptional about being open and honest because my parents did a great job of creating a nonjudgmental, safe home. No matter the problem, joy, or burden, I always felt like I could tell them anything—friends, boys, and school. We really did have great open conversations.

Unfortunately, our family kept quiet when it came to all things regarding my dad and his job. From the time I was a little girl, I was scared for my dad, even frightened for our family. I feared that the evil that my dad encountered on the job would follow him home. At some point, it was just a matter of time before my family or I became a victim.

However, the lie I chose to believe for so long was that I was the only one feeling like this. I thought I was the only one who was afraid for my dad, his life, or our family. I was under the impression that my mom and sister took no issue with what Dad did for work and I was just overreacting by being anxious. I especially never thought my dad was scared or fearful on the job, especially because he did things like run into burning apartments.

How could he be afraid of anything if he did something like that?

Because I thought I was the only one in the family feeling like this, it was easier for me to keep quiet. I didn't want anyone to think I was crazy because, to me, my fears felt so irrational and I was living completely void of faith. However, keeping quiet only made things worse, and when I tried to manage my fears and anxieties, I only magnified them greater. Not to mention the darkness that rolled into our home as a result of my dad's involvement in the apartment fire and large mass murder. It threw my dad's job in our faces, and we were forced to look at it all or choose to live with each other with only surface-deep intimacy.

I also worried about talking to my dad about his job. I didn't want to hurt his feelings. I didn't want him to think that he sacrificed his family's mental health in the process because he chose this profession. My dad is so tender, and I didn't want to see him cry or talk about his feelings because that really just made all of mine more real. I thought that, if I just handled my own fears and anxieties without ever talking to my family, let alone my dad, about how I was feeling, then I was being brave or something. I felt like I was protecting my dad from having to hear about my issues.

A very wise counselor once told us, "What you protect, you make weak."

I was making my dad weak in my eyes. I wasn't giving him the opportunity to walk through my pain with me and allow him to handle it for the grown man that he was.

Talking about my dad's profession wasn't easy, but my family really committed to honesty and safety as we pursued health. The Lord provided an amazing friend, a counselor to help get the conversation going. We needed to expose how we were all feeling and what we could do to support each other. We needed to talk about how it made us all feel when my dad ran into a blazing apartment, knowing the loves of his life were waiting at home for him. We needed to know how my dad was processing the evil he experienced with the man who killed all of his children and how he was attempting to get over that. Really, even though we all needed to talk, the person we needed to hear from the most was my dad.

During the counseling process, I realized that my dad was and is the eternal protector of our family. Unfortunately, when he chose to stay quiet when it came to how he felt, dealt with, and survived his job, he thought he was protecting us girls, but really it was forcing us to fill in our own blanks. None of us had a clue as to how he was feeling and what he went through when he left for work every day. My mom, sister, and I all assumed different things to fill in the silence. I just assumed that my dad was fearless and he would do anything to protect and serve the city he was an officer for. I assumed he was daring, leading me to believe he was careless and didn't consider how his decisions would impact his girls at home.

Why would he risk his life being a police officer if it meant there were always a possibility that he wouldn't come home? Did he even think of what he would be robbing us of? Did he even consider that his family needed him more than the strangers he vowed to protect?

Just as I was protecting him by not wanting him to know how scared I was of his job, he was protecting all of us from his feelings. Or so we all thought. Really, we were all just making each other weak and only deepening the wound of doubt, fear, and anxiety that was created in all of us. Because we let it go for so long, I believe Satan used that as a foothold to bind us to fear for too long.

As my dad began to share how he handled his job, along with the evil he encountered and the hurt he had seen, I realized he was never doing anything on his own. He began to share how his faith in the Lord kept him going. He was never careless or fearless. He just knew that God was in control. He knew he had been called to be an officer and his obedience would allow God to be glorified through him.

He was scared on the job many times, and he never made a decision without thinking about us girls first. His faith was massive. It was so special to hear about my dad's relationship with the Lord because that eventually brought me to a place where I could begin erasing the false beliefs

I had about my Lord and Savior and I could begin filling my heart with His truths.

Only by God's redeeming grace and love for our family that we would begin talking and pursue a health in our family that could never be shaken. Our family is truly built on the rock and steadfast love of Christ, and looking back, we all know that we had to go on this journey separately and as a family to fully let go of the reins of life and allow God to be in control of all of us. It wasn't until we brought our feelings out of the darkness and into the light that God could truly be glorified through our journey.

CHAPTER 7

Where We Are Now

Years have passed since we went through counseling as a family and learned the lessons of communicating in a family as unique as ours. As I write these words, I can't help but see God's grace for our family, my dad, and his profession. I also can't help but see the selfishness that I battled for so long. The root of my anxiety, fear, and then anger was in a place of thinking that I was in control of this life. I thought I could control not only my safety but also the welfare of my dad as he left for work. The selfishness comes from me thinking I could do it better than God Almighty. I'm so thankful for the grace that God gave me as I worked out my false beliefs in Him. I wonder what he thought as he watched me try to control everything around me, only to end up right back where I started, scared and exhausted.

I believe he would stand back and just shake his head with a little smirk, just like my dad would, and say, "I'm here, Meghan. When you're ready, come rest and let me take over."

I have learned a lot about anxiety over my many sessions in counseling. I think it's fascinating that anger usually covers up struggles with anxiety and tries to hide the fear we are refusing to look at. I could safely admit that I had a bit of a temper growing up, and as I grew up, so did the temper. It got bigger and louder as I became an adult. I did not like this quality about myself, but I truly felt like, in the midst of my anger, I could not control my outbursts. My temper would literally take over.

I later learned that my anger was covering up the wounds of anxiety and worry deep within me. It was hard to admit that the fear of my dad's job had manifested into this monster known as anger, that is, rage toward my dad for choosing this profession and the city for being so violent. I had fury for the thoughts I had of him not coming home or the fear of there being a knock at our door with the chief coming to notify us that my dad was killed in the line of duty.

I was also angry with God because my false theology about Him led me to believe that he wasn't capable of keeping my dad safe in our town. Even the world was just too evil. And it was just a matter of time before sin and darkness prevailed against the mighty hand of God.

As I began to recognize that what I believed about God was all wrong, I began to feel shame. I was humbled that it took me so long to get it that God's grace and love for me was enough. Yes, this world is fallen, and sin entered the world with one bite of an apple. Yet, God sacrificed his son so we could be made right again. God was and still is in control of all, and every experience I went through was just part of his master plan so He could be glorified through my life. The same goes for my dad, our family, and everyone.

In God's perfect timing and sovereignty, he got our family talking, and I realized that how I was feeling was anything but crazy. My mom and my sister were scared as well. They thought about the evil in the world and my dad's role in crime. They wondered if he were being safe or not. They thought about if he were thinking about us when he rolled on calls and if he fought to get home safe to us. I was not alone. More powerful than that, as my dad started to talk, my fears and anxieties begun to unravel.

By the grace of God, my dad opened up and let us girls see a little bit of his heart. He shared that he was scared. Not a second went by that he didn't think about his girls. Every time he went on a call, we were in the front of his mind, and he fought with all of his might to come home to us. As he ran into the burning apartment, he thought of the young woman in there and immediately thought of us. If we were in that apartment, he would want someone to come rescue us at any cost. He did risk his life to save others, but he never for a moment stopped thinking about his wife and daughters.

He continued to share how his job was a calling. His character, integrity, selflessness, and heart for the city were a calling from God. He prayed every time he went to work, and his relationship with God was strong. He trusted the Lord that He would work through him to impact our city for good and He would protect his family at home while he served our community. He was scared when he was in danger, but he trusted in the Lord to protect him.

What a powerful example of a Christ follower he was. I am humbled when I thought that my dad was willing to sacrifice his own to life to save another, all to the glory and honor of God.

How healing it was to hear my dad's heart. It was so hard to know how he felt about his profession and even why he chose to be a police officer in the first place. The whys I had wondered for so long were beginning to get answered. His vulnerability allowed us all to understand him better and open the lines of communication so we could all continue to pursue health.

The lesson we learned after so many years of doing life as a family was that silence, not Dad's job, was the enemy. In the silence, evil would get a foothold and begin to rip away at our family, but in the openness, the light of the Lord could shine in the darkness. We could begin to look at my dad's job as the calling that it was, and through that, we could be nothing but proud and honored to be his family.

The blessing in disguise was my dad running into a burning apartment in 2003 and being on the cover of local and national newspapers immediately following the worst mass murder in the history of our town in 2004. Those events were terribly hard to experience as a family, yet, like taking beauty from ashes, God worked in all of us and gave us the ability to heal past wounds, speak up when scared, and begin a new chapter of open communication regarding all things associated with Dad's job.

I think faith is the common denominator that all families with servicepeople have. We cannot control this crazy world. We have to let go of the reins and trust that, as your parent heads to his or her substation, pulls into a firehouse, or boards a plane for overseas, we are not in control. But someone is.

Peace and healing came to our family when we realized that, through all of these years of fear and doubt, God was always in control. He was seated next to my dad in his patrol car, breathing oxygen into his lungs in that fire and weeping for the death of those nine children alongside my father. We have to believe in the higher power of God; otherwise, their professions are too much to bear. When it is too much, we go from pride and honor for our loved ones to resentment, fear, and anger.

What a blessing it has been to grow up and continue developing as my father's daughter. Our journey was (and still is) unique, as he remains an active officer. However, through God's grace, we see the beauty in the sacrifice that is his job. We keep talking and never stop, especially when we are scared. I can only hope and pray that God will be glorified in us sharing our journey so your family can begin to live in the peace and confidence that we have found in the Lord.

I can't help my smile when I think about life behind my dad's shield, all that his badge signifies and represents as he wears it proudly on his chest. I love how my heavenly father also provides a shield in the armor of God. "In all circumstances take up the shield of faith, with which you can extinguish all the flaming darts of the evil one" (Eph. 6:16).

We could not get through this life as a police officer's family without faith. I am so thankful for the shield that my heavenly father provides so I can confidently stand behind my dad's shield.

CONCLUSION

Thank you for allowing me to share my story with you. If you have a parent who is a police officer or works in any other profession that is a little more dangerous than others are, I pray that you cling to the hope and faith of our Lord, Jesus Christ.

God is always there, and He will be glorified through your parent's profession. At times, you will feel overwhelmed or alone in your fears and doubts. But please trust me when I say that you are never alone. God is there with you, using your experience as a family to write your story.

I plead with you to start talking. Ask your parents questions; allow them to ask about you. Leave the lines of communication open. Silence and keeping others in the dark is the enemy, not the profession. Things don't look as scary in the light, so don't be afraid to bring everything out of the darkness.

Also, never be afraid to ask for help. There are so many wonderful counselors in this world that I believe God has gifted them to help us be free from our bondage. Our family could not have attained help without counseling. They helped us know what questions to ask each other, how to handle life around us, and how to cope with the very real fear and anxiety that would well up inside us. There is no shame in asking for help, so please lean on the resources around you.

Men and women who serve and protect others are all heroes in my book. They follow a calling that is bigger than all of us. Yes, when they go to work, they put themselves into situations that are dangerous, but they serve knowing that the King of Kings is right there with them. They are brave and selfless, and they are willing to lay down their lives for others, which is what we are called to do in the first place, isn't it? What an honor it is to be their children and walk this faith journey of life alongside them.

CPSIA information can be obtained at www.ICGtesting.com
Printed in the USA
BVOW030323250413

319049BV00002B/3/P